WESLEY R. WILLIS

VICTOR BOOKS®

A DIVISION OF SCRIPTURE PRESS PUBLICATIONS INC.
USA CANADA ENGLAND

Recommended Dewey Decimal Classification: 227.5
Suggested Subject Heading: BIBLE, N.T.—EPHESIANS

Library of Congress Catalog Card Number: 87-081027
ISBN: 0-89693-770-4

VICTOR BOOKS
A division of SP Publications, Inc.
        Wheaton, Illinos 60187

CONTENTS

How to Use This Study

Personal Growth Bible Studies are designed to help you understand God's Word and how it applies to everyday life. To complete the studies in this book, you will need to use a Bible. A good modern translation of the Bible, such as the *New International Version* or the *New American Standard Bible*, will give you the most help. (NOTE: the questions in this book are based on the *New International Version.*)

You will find it helpful to follow a similar sequence with each study. First, read the introductory paragraphs. This material helps set the tone and lay the groundwork for the passage to be studied. Once you have completed this part of the study, spend time reading the assigned passage in your Bible. This will give you a general feel for the contents of the passage.

Having completed the preliminaries, you are then ready to dig deeper into the Scripture passage. Each study is divided into several sections so that you can take a close-up look at the smaller parts of the larger passage. These sections each begin with a synopsis of the Scripture to be studied in that section. Following each synopsis is a two-part study section made up of *Explaining the Text* and *Examining the Text.*

Explaining the Text gives background notes and commentary to help you understand points in the text that may not be readily apparent. After reading any comments that appear in *Explaining the Text*, answer each question under *Examining the Text.*

At the end of each study is a section called *Experiencing the Text.* The questions in this section focus on the application of biblical principles to life. You may find that some of the questions can be answered immediately; others will require that you spend more time reflecting on the passages you have just studied.

The distinctive format of the Personal Growth Bible Studies make them easy to use individually as well as for group study. If the majority of those in your group answer the questions before the group meeting, spend most of your time together discussing the *Experiencing* questions. If, on the other hand, members have not answered the questions ahead of time and you have adequate time in your group meeting, work through all of the questions together.

However you use this series of studies, our prayer is that you will understand the Bible as never before, and that because of this understanding, you will experience a rich and dynamic Christian life. If questions of interpretation arise in the course of this study, we recommend you refer to the two-volume set, *The Bible Knowledge Commentary*, edited by John F. Walvoord and Roy B. Zuck (Victor Books, 1984, 1986).

—

Introduction to the Epistle to the Ephesians

Who was Paul? We first meet Paul in Acts 7:58 where he is called "Saul." In this initial encounter, Saul is mentioned as an observer at the execution of Stephen, a leader in the Jerusalem church. Saul, according to Acts 9, had set out to completely eradicate Christianity. He was going from city to city, with letters of authorization, searching for Christians and carting them off to jail.

Saul's whole life was redirected when he encountered Jesus on the road to Damascus. After his marvelous conversion, Saul became known as Paul. He then began to promote Christianity with the same ardor that he had previously opposed it.

Why did he write Ephesians? Paul visited Ephesus briefly at the end of his second missionary journey. He then lived in Ephesus for several years during his third journey. The Letter to the Ephesians was written to help reinforce the excellent start that the Ephesian believers had made. Many feel that this letter, written while Paul was in prison (ca. A.D. 60) was intended to be read by believers in several surrounding cities, as well as those in Ephesus.

The Epistle to the Ephesians was written to be circulated and read in the churches of Asia Minor—near the northeastern shores of the Mediterranean (present-day Turkey). It was written to non-Jewish believers and is, thereby, one of the easiest New Testament writings to apply to the church today.

Ephesians is somewhat unique in that there seems to be no particular doctrinal error or relational problem that Paul was trying to correct. Rather, the letter presents the basic foundation of Christianity, and then shows how this foundation is to be applied in the life of the community.

Chapters 1–3 describe the believer's position in Christ and the spiritual resources available to every Christian. The second half of the book, chapters 4–6, presents a practical explanation of how we should live because of that position. Paul clearly demonstrates that there is nothing quite so practical as sound doctrine.

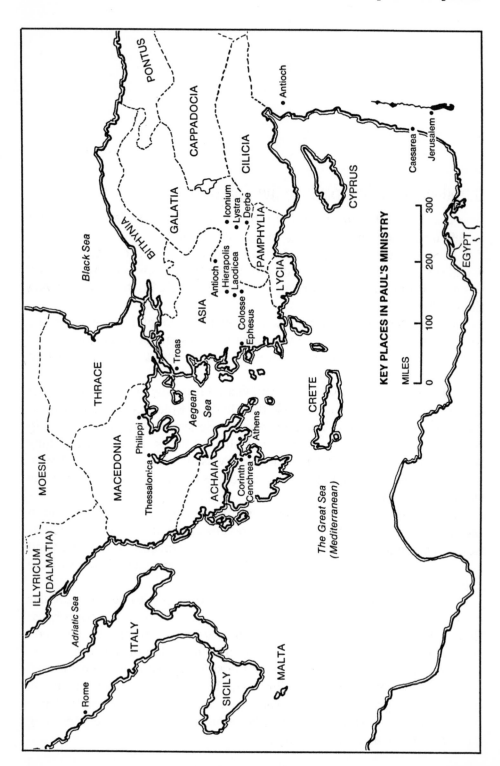

KEY PLACES IN PAUL'S MINISTRY

Ephesians 1:1-14

New Blessings in Christ

The deceased millionaire, Howard Hughes, holds a bizarre fascination for many. His incredibly eccentric lifestyle, his compulsive seclusion as he approached the end of his life, and the absence of a will after his death all add to the mysterious aura. Though worth millions of dollars, Hughes reportedly withdrew to the shadowy confines of his bedroom, living solely on soft drinks and prepackaged cupcakes. His twilight existence gave no indication of the abundant resources at his disposal.

We can only shake our heads in disbelief and wonder what mental aberration could bring a man to such a state—fabulously wealthy and yet starving in isolation. Unfortunately, some Christians are guilty of similar behavior. When God brings us into His family, we immediately become heir to a spiritual fortune. However, though God has blessed us with untold spiritual wealth, many ignore those resources, choosing rather to lead lives of frustration and defeat. A believer who fails to recognize those resources, enjoys little more than spiritual bankruptcy.

In this first section of Ephesians, Paul provides an accounting of the spiritual blessings that we inherit due to our new position in Christ. As we examine these blessings in greater detail, may our lives be full and rich, a testimony of our position as heirs to a spiritual fortune in Christ Jesus.

A. GOD HAS BLESSED US IN CHRIST *(Eph. 1:1-3).*   This book begins with an identification of the author (Paul the Apostle), the recipients (Ephesian believers), and an affirmation of the fact that salvation includes a wide range of spiritual blessings.

Examining the Text	*Explaining the Text*
1. Read Ephesians 1:1-3. Who called Paul to become an apostle? (v. 1)	1. The word *apostle* means "sent one." In the New Testament it is used of certain church leaders who had seen Christ personally.
Why would Paul stress his calling at the beginning of the chapter?	
2. How does Paul's use of the word *saint* (v. 1) differ from popular usage today?	2. As Paul used the word, *saints* (literally "holy ones") refers to all who believe in Christ and have been born again through faith in Christ.
If we really think of ourselves as saints, how will it affect the way we live?	
3. According to verse 3, what kinds of blessings has God given to us? (v. 3)	3. Paul wrote verse 3 as a preface to verses 4-14. Verse 3 introduces the subject, spiritual blessings. Verses 4-14 provide a full description of these spiritual blessings.

B. GOD SAVED US *(Eph. 1:4-8)*.   Not only has God provided salvation, but believers also receive forgiveness of their sin. Other riches include abundant spiritual wisdom and understanding.

Explaining the Text	*Examining the Text*
1. Notice that when God determined people would be saved (1:4), He called them holy and blameless. This doesn't mean they automatically behave that way, but God views them like this based on Christ's righteousness.	1. Read Ephesians 1:4-8. When did God establish His plan for the salvation of humankind? (v. 4)
	2. What does the concept of adoption communicate about our relationship with God through Jesus Christ? (v. 5)
	3. In what ways does our salvation bring praise to God?
4. It is important to recognize that our salvation was made possible only by Christ's death.	4. List the things we have received in Christ according to verses 7 and 8.

Examining the Text	*Explaining the Text*
On what basis have we received them? (v. 7)	
5. According to verse 8, how would you describe God's attitude in giving spiritual blessings to us?	

C. GOD GUIDES US *(Eph. 1:9-12).*   Part of the understanding that believers receive is the revelation of God's will. Not only can we know God's purpose, we can also see how God is accomplishing it through Jesus Christ.

Examining the Text	*Explaining the Text*
1. What mystery has God made known to us? (vv. 9-10)	1. A "mystery" is something that we could not know unless God specifically revealed it to us. The revelation of the church, Jew and Gentile becoming one, is the mystery Paul shares.
2. When will all of the various elements in God's plan finally come to fruition and be understood? (v. 10)	

Explaining the Text	Examining the Text
3. Notice that God is not disinterested in what is happening in the world. He is actively involved in accomplishing His will.	3. What was Paul's expectation about the probability of God's will being accomplished in the world? (v. 11) 4. What "benefit" comes to God as a result of our response to Jesus Christ? (v. 12)

D. GOD SEALED US *(Eph. 1:13-14).*   When we placed our faith in Christ, we received the Holy Spirit. Though the bulk of our inheritance is future, the Holy Spirit testifies to the fact that we will receive it.

Explaining the Text	Examining the Text
	1. Read Ephesians 1:13-14. What must happen before a person can believe in Jesus Christ? (v. 13)
2. A deposit is similar to earnest money given when signing a contract. It is evidence that all of the terms of the contract will be met—that the individual will follow through on his promise.	2. What is the seal (deposit) that has been given to those who believe? (v. 13)

Examining the Text	*Explaining the Text*
3. What is the full inheritance of the believer? (v. 14)	

Experiencing the Text

1. Since we, as believers, are holy and blameless in our standing before God, what difference should it make in our actions and attitudes toward other Christians with whom we live and worship?

2. What are some things we can do to bring praise and glory to God each day?

3. God offers us salvation through His Son Jesus Christ, but we must accept this gift. If you have accepted salvation, write a brief prayer of thanksgiving. If you have not yet accepted Jesus Christ, but would like to, write out and then pray a prayer thanking God for this gift and telling Him that you now accept Jesus.

Ephesians 1:15-23

New Wisdom in Christ

When my family and I moved into our present house, every new day was an adventure. Each time we entered a room we discovered things that we had not realized before. Some parts of the house were just what we had expected. But others were totally different. Interestingly, some of the things that we now enjoy most about our house are things that seemed relatively minor in our initial evaluation.

Through the years, we have become quite comfortable and accustomed to the features of this house. We now take for granted the things that amazed and amused us initially. We don't even notice many things that a visitor might observe immediately.

This fact became obvious to us recently when Elaine and I did a critical "walk-through" of our house. We looked at each room to see just what repairs or maintenance were needed. The chips, nicks, spots, and other needed repairs have filled our "job jar" to overflowing.

In many ways the Christian life is similar. At first, everything is new and every discovery exciting. For new Christians, this section of Ephesians describes key features of our life in Christ. But for those of us who have been saved for some time, this section is different. It reminds us of things that we may be taking for granted. Whether we are new or seasoned Christians, the implications of our salvation are exciting.

A. FAITHFUL PRAYING FOR OTHER CHRISTIANS *(Eph. 1:15-16)*.   This section begins with Paul describing his ministry to the Ephesian Christians. After hearing of their spiritual growth, Paul prayed regularly for them.

Examining the Text	*Explaining the Text*
1. Read Ephesians 1:15-16. What two relationships in the Christian life was Paul concerned about? (v. 15)	1. The phrase, "For this reason" (v. 15), which introduces this section, probably refers back to spiritual blessings in verse 3.
2. How is faith in Jesus Christ related to "love for all the saints"? (v. 15)	
3. Why was Paul giving thanks to God for the Ephesians? (v. 16)	3. "I have not stopped giving thanks" does not mean praying 24 hours a day. It indicates regular, systematic prayer.

B. THE IMPORTANCE OF WISDOM *(Eph. 1:17)*.   One of the main requests that Paul made for the Ephesians was that they would mature spiritually and come to know Christ better. This would come through the Holy Spirit's ministry to them.

Examining the Text	*Explaining the Text*
1. Read Ephesians 1:17. What attributes does Paul ascribe to God in verse 17?	

Explaining the Text	Examining the Text
2. Revelation usually refers to the knowledge of facts or truths that we have because God has told us in the Bible. Wisdom is how to use or apply that knowledge.	2. For a Christian, what should be the relationship between wisdom and revelation? (v. 17) 3. According to Paul, what should be the result of acquiring wisdom through revelation? (v. 17)

C. THE IMPORTANCE OF SPIRITUAL UNDERSTANDING *(Eph. 1:18-21).* Paul prayed that the Ephesians would have spiritual insight to understand their hope, their wealth, and the power that God demonstrated through Christ.

Explaining the Text	Examining the Text
1. Paul's prayer, "that the eyes of your heart may be enlightened," refers to understanding spiritual truth.	1. Read Ephesians 1:18-21. What three things did Paul pray would result from having the eyes of their hearts enlightened? (vv. 18-19) 2. What example did Paul use in verses 19-20 to help explain the extent of God's great power?

Examining the Text	Explaining the Text
How might this power be manifest in our lives today?	
3. Describe how you feel about who Christ is, and the position that He has, when you read verses 20-21.	3. According to these verses, there is no position or power that is greater than that assigned to Christ.

D. THE EXTENT OF CHRIST'S AUTHORITY *(Eph. 1:22-23).* God, through His power, has assigned to Christ a position of power and authority. Christ's authority is particularly important to the Church because He is our Head.

Examining the Text	Explaining the Text
1. Read Ephesians 1:22-23. What are two ways in which God's power is seen in Jesus Christ? (v. 22)	1. Verses 22-23 explain and expand on the topic of the power of God which Paul wanted the Ephesians to recognize.
2. What do you think it means that all things have been placed under the feet of Christ?	

Explaining the Text	*Examining the Text*
3. Headship can imply two things—authority and giving direction. Both may be included here.	3. What are some implications of the fact that Christ is the Head of the Church?
	4. In what way does Christ fill "everything in every way"?

Experiencing the Text

1. How should our relationship with God affect the way that we respond to fellow believers?

2. Make a list of fellow believers and specific requests you would like to pray for this week.

Experiencing the Text

3. What steps can you take to develop a closer relationship with God?

4. What steps can you take to rely more on God's "great power for us who believe"?

Ephesians 2:1-10

New Life in Christ

It is easy to forget that two totally different systems are at work in the world. And these are in direct conflict with each other. We forget, even though we know, that God and Satan have nothing in common—that good and evil, light and dark, righteousness and unrighteousness are never in agreement. And because we forget, often we assume that there is a vast middle ground.

Scripture reveals that there is no neutral ground. One is either for God or opposed to Him. Paul describes these two systems in this first part of Ephesians 2. We all operated on the basis of Satan's system before we were saved—before we were made alive in Christ. But now that we have been born again, we should be operating on the basis of God's direction.

Of course, this means constant spiritual conflict because so much of what goes on around us is under Satan's direction. We need only to listen carefully to popular music, or watch almost any popular TV show to become keenly aware of that conflict. Most of what is communicated through the media reflects distinctly anti-Christian values. And that means those presentations communicate principles that are appropriate to Satan's goals rather than God's. Paul's instruction in this section explains to us how we can live lives that glorify God through the power of His Holy Spirit. This is the power that made us "alive with Christ even when we were dead in transgressions."

A. LIVING AS DEAD PEOPLE *(Eph. 2:1-3).*   Before we become Christians, we are spiritually dead in sin. Our attitudes and actions are driven by earthly, physical desires which reflect Satan's purposes in the world.

Examining the Text	*Explaining the Text*
1. Read Ephesians 2:1-3. What are the characteristics of a person who is not alive spiritually? (vv. 1-2)	1. In contrasting physical and spiritual life, Paul explained that although people may be alive physically (2:2), if unsaved, they are dead spiritually (2:1).
2. What is the relationship between Satan and "the ways of this world"?	2. Satan is the "ruler of the kingdom of the air."
3. According to verse 3, what is the lifestyle of those who are dead in their trespasses and sins?	
In what ways should the lifestyle of a Christian be different?	
4. What did we deserve for following Satan, and for the way that we once lived? (v. 3)	4. The phrase, "We were by nature objects of wrath" (i.e., of God's wrath), is a Hebrew idiom asserting the essential depravity of human nature. This seems to indicate that everyone, Jew and Gentile alike, stands guilty before God.

B. RECEIVING LIFE THROUGH CHRIST *(Eph. 2:4-7)*.   As an expression of His love, God offers us life, saving us through His grace. To His great glory, God's provision for us is a treasure of immeasurable value, available only through Jesus Christ.

Explaining the Text	*Examining the Text*
	1. Read Ephesians 2:4-7. Why do you think God's love for us is so great? (v. 4)
2. "Grace" is God giving us something we don't deserve. "Mercy" is God *not* giving us what we *do* deserve.	2. Contrast what God has given us (vv. 4-5) with what we deserve to be given (v. 3). In what ways has God been merciful to us?
3. The phrase, "It is by grace you have been saved," is used parenthetically in verse 5.	3. What three things did God do for us as He demonstrated His great love in mercy? (vv. 5-6)
4. The word *kindness* can include the idea of generosity and/or goodness.	4. Why did God demonstrate His love for us so graciously? (v. 7)

C. LIVING TO GOD'S GLORY *(Eph. 2:8-10)*. We always must re-
member that salvation is God's work and not our own so that we cannot
brag about it. Since we have been saved, it is our obligation to live in such
a way that our good works glorify God. This is what God planned for us
long before we were saved.

Examining the Text	*Explaining the Text*
1. Read Ephesians 2:8-10. According to verse 8, what is the means of our salvation?	1. Verses 8 and 9 elaborate on the parenthetical phrase in verse 5, "It is by grace you are saved."
2. What did we have to do in order to be saved? (vv. 8-9)	
3. What should be the proper relationship between faith and works in the Christian life? (vv. 8-10)	3. We are not able to do anything (work) to achieve our salvation, but it is a gift we need only accept.
4. What is meant by the phrase, "We are God's workmanship"? (v. 10)	4. "Workmanship" also can be translated "creation."

Explaining the Text	Examining the Text
5. Even though we are saved by faith, not works, works are an important expression after we have been saved.	5. What should we do because of the fact that we have been saved? (v. 10)
	6. When did God determine that we should do good works? (v. 10)

Experiencing the Text

1. What can we do to resist unconsciously absorbing attitudes and copying the actions of those who follow "the ruler of the kingdom of the air"?

2. How should we respond to God in light of His great mercy expressed through His grace?

Experiencing the Text

3. What can we do that will contribute to demonstrating the "incomparable riches of His grace"?

4. What are some reasons that a Christian might fail to live as God expects (doing good works)?

Ephesians 2:11-22

New Relationships in Christ

Science, technology, and human ingenuity are wonderful. Every day we discover ways in which our lives can be made easier or more productive. Not only are we making marvelous discoveries and finding new ways to apply them, but products employing those discoveries are getting to the marketplace more quickly than ever before.

And yet conflicts, hostility, and broken relationships also are thriving. The daily newspaper can be very depressing reading. Terrorism, crime, and international conflict seem to dominate the news. Violence surrounds us, both in the form of aimless expressions of frustration or anger, and in coldly calculated attacks against specific persons or groups.

Much of the violence is motivated by religious fervor. Some of the most brutal wars in history were at least partially the result of religious disputes. Even today, religious issues are the source of much of the conflict that contributes to worldwide tension.

Whether it be the continuing saga of conflict in the Middle East or bombings and shootings in Northern Ireland, the religious motivation is unmistakable. Yet when a person becomes a member of God's family through faith in Jesus Christ, love rather than hatred should result. When love becomes the motivating factor, old conflicts and hostility are eliminated.

While "religion" alienates and divides people, biblical Christianity promotes peace and produces new unity. Instead of hating and fighting each other, those who have been in conflict are brought together into a single body, the body of Christ. This body grows and matures to the glory of God.

A. HOPELESS SEPARATION *(Eph. 2:11-12).*   Before placing their faith
in Christ, Gentiles (the uncircumcised) were alienated from Israel (the
circumcised) and from God. Their situation was hopeless, isolated from
God and from His blessings.

Examining the Text	*Explaining the Text*
1. Read Ephesians 2:11-12. The word *therefore* (v. 11) refers back to the previous section. That means that what Paul is about to say is built on the point he has just made. Reread 2:1-10 and summarize in a sentence or two the main idea of that section.	1. This section contrasts Jew with Gentile, emphasizing their former differences which produced alienation.
2. What barriers separated Gentiles from Jews? (vv. 11-12)	
3. What were the consequences of being a Gentile and not being part of the nation of Israel? (v. 12)	3. While some Gentiles joined the nation of Israel as proselytes, most Gentiles were totally separated from God.
4. How do you think the Gentile Christians felt when they heard verses 11 and 12 read aloud for the first time?	

B. JOYFUL RECONCILIATION *(Eph. 2:13).* Jesus Christ, through His sacrificial death, enables those who were separate and alienated to come to God.

Explaining the Text	*Examining the Text*
1. The phrase, "But now" (v. 13) points back to the word "formerly" (v. 11). These phrases are used to contrast the former status of the Gentile believers ("separated") with their new status ("brought near").	1. Read Ephesians 2:13. To whom is Paul referring in the phrase, "You who once were far away"? (v. 13) How were they "brought near" (reconciled) to God? (v. 13)
2. The alienation that the Ephesians experienced prior to salvation left them without hope. The "blood of Christ" (v. 13) refers to Jesus' sacrificial death by which reconciliation was made possible.	2. In this passage, Paul describes reconciliation as being "brought near" to God. Paul discussed this same concept throughout his New Testament letters. Read the Scripture passages listed below and jot down the words or phrases that Paul uses in those verses to describe or define reconciliation. Romans 5:6-11 2 Corinthians 5:14-21 Colossians 1:21-23

C. UNITY IN CHRIST *(Eph. 2:14-18).* Jesus brought peace by destroying the wall between Jew and Gentile, and establishing a new entity, the church. As a result, we all have equal access to God through faith in Jesus Christ.

Examining the Text

1. Read Ephesians 2:14-18. What barrier has been removed so that Jew and Gentile could become one?

2. What is the "new man" that Paul refers to in verse 15?

3. How and why was the barrier separating Jew and Gentile destroyed? (vv. 15-16)

4. In what areas has a new relationship and a new unity been established? (vv. 15-16)

5. By what means do both Jew and Gentile have access to the Father? (vv. 17-18)

Explaining the Text

1. The phrase, "dividing wall of hostility" (v. 14), is a metaphor describing all that separated Jew and Gentile. The metaphor owes its force to the wall in the temple area of Jerusalem which separated the court of the Gentiles (the outermost court) from the inner courts (open only to Jews).

2. The Greek word *kainon* (translated "new," v. 15) means new in character or quality as opposed to new in time.

4. The Mosaic Law was given to Israel (613 regulations made up of the Commandments, the Statutes, and the Ordinances). While the moral intent certainly continues, the Mosaic System was done away with at Christ's death (cp. Gal. 3:23-25).

5. Before Christ's death, Gentiles came to God only by identifying with Israel. Now both Jew and Gentile come directly through Christ.

D. POSITION IN GOD'S FAMILY *(Eph. 2:19-22).* Now all believers are part of the same group, the church. But what is the church? The church is built on the teachings of the apostles and prophets (Jesus Christ is the very Cornerstone of this teaching). The church is not a building made of wood, brick, or stone; it is all believers joined together in Him. As believers grow together, they become the very dwelling place of God's Spirit.

Explaining the Text	*Examining the Text*
	1. Read Ephesians 2:19-22. List the words and/or phrases used to describe the Gentiles before and after they became Christians.
2. A cornerstone is used to assure a level foundation. In ancient buildings, the entire structure was lined up with the chief cornerstone. Thus, its placement was crucial.	2. Note the imagery Paul uses to describe the church. Using your imagination, explore more fully the metaphors Paul employs in verses 19-22—kingdom, family, temple. How is the church like (or unlike) the picture Paul paints of it?
	3. How do you think additions are made to this holy temple so that it continues to rise? (v. 21)
4. Rather than residing in a physical tabernacle or temple, God's Spirit now indwells believers (who are God's true house).	4. What do these verses suggest about relationships between Christians? (vv. 21-22)

Experiencing the Text

1. Within modern culture, what are some of the identifiable groups that are hated by other groups?

What are the reasons given for this hostility?

2. How could a genuine relationship with Christ relieve this hostility?

How should this affect your life and relationships on a personal level?

3. What are some of the practical implications of the fact that all of us who are Christians have been "brought near" (reconciled) to God?

Experiencing the Text

4. In what ways can we experience peace in our lives through the work of Christ?

In what ways have you personally experienced this peace?

5. Think back on the imagery Paul uses to describe the church. How do these images affect your life? What does it mean for you to be a citizen of God's kingdom?

What does it mean for you to be a member of God's family?

What does it mean for you to be joined with other Christians as part of God's temple?

Ephesians 3:1-13

New Organism: The Body of Christ

The story is told about two small churches in a very small town. For years these churches had competed for the few townspeople who attended church regularly. Finally someone suggested that rather than constantly struggling to outdo each other, they should merge into one reasonably good-sized congregation.

Most felt that this was an appropriate solution, and so a committee was appointed to work out the details of the merger. The committee resolved many differences quite easily, and it appeared as though they would accomplish the transition with little trauma.

But then a disagreement surfaced. Each congregation recited the Lord's Prayer in the morning worship service. Unfortunately, they recited different versions. One prayed "forgive us our debts as we forgive our debtors," while the other asked "forgive us our trespasses as we forgive those who trespass against us." While this seems to be a relatively minor variation, each congregation wanted to retain its version of the prayer. And the longer they worked to resolve the problem, the more each side became hardened and resistant to change. The disagreement became so intense, that the appointed committee decided consolidation was impossible.

A brief notice in the local newspaper recounted the aborted attempt at consolidation. The newspaper's account explained the various issues surrounding the disagreement and the churches' inability to resolve it. The article concluded with this insightful remark: "After abandoning all hope of resolving the conflict, one church returned to its debts and the other to its trespasses."

How common such attitudes are among Christians. We forget all that we have in common, and allow minor differences to paralyze us. But Paul clearly teaches in this section of Ephesians that we are "one body" in Jesus Christ. And this unity should enable us to represent Him effectively in the world.

A. REVELATION OF THE CHURCH *(Eph. 3:1-6)*. In His grace, God revealed to Paul that during this age He was going to use a different means to express His eternal plan in the world. Through Christ, both Jew and Gentile are brought together into one new entity, the church.

Examining the Text	Explaining the Text
1. Read Ephesians 3:1-6. The phrase, "For this reason" directs our attention back to a previous point. Reread 2:11-22 and summarize the main point of that passage.	
2. To what group of people did Paul primarily direct his preaching?	2. The Ephesians had worshiped idols before responding to Paul's proclamation of the Gospel of Christ.
3. What do you think Paul meant when he described himself as a "prisoner of Christ Jesus"? (v. 1)	
4. What was Paul able to understand through special insight? (vv. 3-4)	4. God's grace (which always has been operative in the world) was administered in the present church age first through Paul and then through the church.

Explaining the Text	Examining the Text
5. A mystery, in the biblical sense, is something that could not and had not been known before God specifically revealed it.	5. Who, besides Paul, was able to understand "the mystery"? (v. 5)
	6. How was this mystery revealed? (v. 5)
7. The mystery, revealed to Paul, is that both Jew and Gentile could become one in the church.	7. List the three major truths that are included in this mystery (v. 6).

B. PAUL'S CONTRIBUTION TO BUILDING THE CHURCH *(Eph. 3:7-9).* Paul's ministry was to take the marvelous truth of the Gospel to the Gentiles, though he felt unworthy of the honor. While the inclusion of the Gentiles has always been a part of God's eternal plan, it had not been revealed previously. God commissioned Paul to communicate this truth clearly.

Explaining the Text	Examining the Text
	1. Read Ephesians 3:7-9. Based on Paul's references to himself in verses 1-13, what can you say about Paul?

Examining the Text	*Explaining the Text*
2. What might it mean that Paul was a "servant of this gospel"?	2. In verse 7, the word translated "servant" does not mean a slave, but one who provides service, such as a waiter.
3. What insight does verse 7 give us regarding Paul's spirit and attitude?	
4. What are some of the reasons that Paul might have considered himself "less than the least of all God's people"? (v. 8)	4. Paul's humility apparently grew out of an awareness that his success came from God's power working through him.
5. As a servant of the gospel, what two responsibilities were given to Paul? (vv. 8-9)	
6. What information in verse 9 helps us understand the "mystery" of the church?	6. Even though Paul was sent primarily to Gentiles, he was concerned about everyone hearing the gospel.

C. GOD'S PURPOSE FOR THE CHURCH *(Eph. 3:10-13)*. God intends for everyone to know what He is accomplishing. Through Christ, we can come to God freely and confidently.

Explaining the Text	*Examining the Text*
1. The word *manifold* means, literally, "multicolored." The phrase, "manifold wisdom of God" probably refers to the "mystery"—Jew and Gentile becoming one in the church.	1. Read Ephesians 3:10-13. What is the purpose of the church according to verse 10?
	2. Who needs to know about the "manifold wisdom of God"? (v. 10)
3. Christ's death was not some last-minute adjustment, but the key to God's plan from eternity past.	3. Who is the focal point of God's eternal purpose? (v. 11)
4. Because of Christ's death, everyone has free access to God, if they come through Jesus Christ.	4. By what means may we approach God? (v. 12)
	5. For you, what does it mean to approach God with freedom and confidence?

Examining the Text

6. Why do you think that Paul might have feared that the Ephesians were discouraged? (v. 13)

Explaining the Text

6. Some Jews did not want Paul to preach to the Gentiles; and unsaved Gentiles did not like it that so many of their kinsmen turned to Christ.

Experiencing the Text

1. If your church is functioning according to Paul's directives in Ephesians 3:1-13, what qualities or traits should characterize it?

2. Why is unity so difficult to maintain?

3. It's important to realize that we demonstrate proper attitudes through our actions. What actions can you take this week to demonstrate an attitude of love and unity toward other Christians?

Experiencing the Text

4. Why is the church, the body of Christ, so crucial to God's plan for the world?

5. What part do you play in the body of Christ? What part do you play in God's eternal plan?

6. Since we can approach God freely and confidently, what traits should characterize our prayer lives? Our evangelistic efforts?

   What steps will you take to improve the quality of your prayer life and evangelistic efforts?

Ephesians 3:14-21

New Power in Christ

The very mention of the word *housekeeping* strikes terror in the hearts of some people. These people are compulsive about cleanliness. A speck of dust, a cobweb, or a magazine out of place is, to them, a reflection of total depravity. While some maintain that cleanliness is next to godliness, these people put it ahead of godliness. They are the ones whose houses look like you could eat off the floor.

And then there are those whose homes look as if someone *has been* eating off the floor. To these people, house cleaning means rearranging the piles. The patterns in the dust serve as guides to where the piles actually belong.

Somewhere between these two extremes is a balance. Elaine and I feel that we are working to achieve this balance. Of course, our decision to have a neat, clean (but not compulsively clean) house may be a pragmatic decision. With three sons involved in many activities, including interscholastic sports, "compulsively neat" was not an option. At least not if we wished to maintain our sanity.

Elaine and some of her close friends often compare notes on the difficulty of maintaining balance in the mundane world of housekeeping. One year for Christmas one of these friends gave Elaine a framed motto which pictured a somewhat disheveled woman slumped in an easy chair. Below the picture was the phrase, "The secret of perfect housekeeping: very low standards." As you can imagine, this was a cherished gift from a dear friend.

Unfortunately, many apply a similar philosophy to living the Christian life. They set very low standards so that they have little to live up to. The problem with this approach is that God has already set the standards. God's expectations for believers, as described in Ephesians 3:14-21, grow out of who He is and what Christ has done.

A. PRAYER FOR SPIRITUAL STRENGTH *(Eph. 3:14-17a).*   Paul shares with the Ephesian believers his prayer for them, knowing that God's riches are available to His children. Paul specifically prayed that believers would experience the power that comes through giving Christ total possession of their lives.

Examining the Text	*Explaining the Text*
1. Read Ephesians 3:14-17a. What does the phrase, "I kneel before the Father," indicate about Paul's attitude toward God? (v. 14)	1. While standing was the most common posture for praying in the Old Testament, Paul suggests another position.
2. What is the relationship between God and the church, the body of Christ? (v. 15)	
3. What resources does God draw on to provide us with power? (v. 16)	3. When we refer to resources, we commonly think of material blessings. The focus here is on spiritual resources.
4. What do you think Paul meant when he expressed a desire for the Ephesians to be strengthened in their "inner being"? (v. 16)	

Explaining the Text	Examining the Text
5. The word *dwell* is not used to emphasize physical location, rather it connotes possession or control.	5. What qualities would characterize someone who has Christ possessing ("dwelling in") his or her heart? (v. 17)

B. PRAYER TO EXPERIENCE GOD'S LOVE FULLY *(Eph. 3:17b-19)*. Paul also prayed that believers, being grounded in the love of Christ, might grasp the scope of that love. We cannot understand this love except through God's revelation.

Explaining the Text	Examining the Text
1. In the context of verse 17, the word *established* means having "a firm foundation." It probably refers back to 2:20-22 where the church is described as a strong building.	1. Read Ephesians 3:17b-19. What are two ways in which Paul pictures (represents) believers? (Note the verbs used in verse 17b.)
	2. What are the four dimensions of the love of Christ that Paul describes in verse 18?
3. Notice that Paul prayed for the Ephesians to have power to understand (grasp) the love of Christ (3:18), and to experience (know) that love which surpasses knowledge (3:19).	3. What do you think Paul intended to emphasize by using physical dimensions to describe an abstract concept such as love? (v. 18)

Examining the Text	Explaining the Text
4. What are some of the practical implications of having a fuller comprehension of Christ's love? (v. 19)	
5. To what extent can a believer be filled with the love of God? (v. 19)	5. The "fullness of God" apparently refers to His nature and attributes.

C. DOXOLOGY OF PRAISE *(Eph. 3:20-21)*.   Paul concludes his prayer with a glorious doxology to God. Paul praises God for what He does in our lives and for how His power works within us. And Paul prays that glory might come to God through Jesus Christ and through His body, the church, forever.

Examining the Text	Explaining the Text
1. Read Ephesians 3:20-21. In many churches, verses 20-21 are set to music and sung as a doxology. What do you see in them that makes them doxological?	1. *Doxology* is a word built from two Greek words meaning "glory" and "words."
2. List some examples of how we expect far less than God is able to accomplish (v. 20).	2. We are finite while God is infinite. Our levels of expectation are finite also.

Explaining the Text	*Examining the Text*
	3. How can we raise our expectation levels to agree more fully with God's power?
4. While it is our responsibility to glorify God, we are not left to our own strength and wisdom in fulfilling this duty.	4. What means does God use to accomplish His will in the world? (v. 20)
	5. What impact do fighting and controversy among Christians have on the glory that God receives? (v. 21)
6. This doxology concludes not only the immediate section (3:14-21), but also the first half (chapters 1–3) of Ephesians.	6. How long will God continue to receive glory? (v. 21)

Experiencing the Text

1. What are some obvious areas of life in which we need spiritual power as we live and serve God today?

2. If you truly allowed Christ to dwell in (completely possess) your heart, how would your life change?

3. What steps can you take to gain a fuller understanding of Christ's love?

4. In what areas do you think God's qualities or attributes need to be experienced more fully in your life?

Experiencing the Text

5. In what ways do your interactions with other believers glorify God?

6. Write out Ephesians 3:20-21 below. Use these verses as your own personal prayer to God.

Ephesians 4:1-16

Believers Ministering Faithfully

Several years ago, a well-known college football coach, returning to campus with his team, was asked a very unusual question by a reporter. "Tell me coach," the reporter asked, "what do you think football has done to improve the physical condition of America?"

"It has done absolutely nothing," the coach replied. "I define football as twenty-two men on the field desperately needing rest, and twenty-two thousand in the stands desperately needing exercise."

This perceptive response certainly was unexpected, but its logic is inescapable. What we needed then, and continue to need, is not another opportunity to watch superb athletes expend great physical energy. We need to burn some calories ourselves. And sitting on the sidelines, munching hot dogs and peanuts is counterproductive.

The church faces a similar dilemma. We have a few players on the field desperately needing rest, with the vast majority sitting in the stands watching. As I travel I meet many pastors and other church leaders. Their most common pleas for help revolve around the problem of recruiting workers. Too few people are doing too many jobs. And too many people are watching them.

Christianity is not a spectator activity. It assumes involvement and participation by every member of Christ's body. Ephesians 4:1-16 is the classic passage describing the nature and strategy of the church. Though we have much in common, we all have unique contributions. And only as everyone works, will the body grow and thrive.

A. UNITY IN CHRIST'S BODY *(Eph. 4:1-6).* As believers, we have an obligation to live out the doctrine that Paul communicated in the first three chapters of his letter to the Ephesians. We are to work at building and maintaining a strong, healthy church. This is made easier by the fact that we have seven significant elements in common.

Examining the Text	*Explaining the Text*
1. Since the word *then* refers back to chapters 1–3, it is important to understand these chapters. Briefly review them and write down several main ideas from Ephesians 1–3.	1. The word *then,* better translated "therefore," is used to introduce the second half of Ephesians. This half of the letter explains *how* to live in accordance with our high position in Christ.
2. Read Ephesians 4:1-6. How does Paul describe himself in verse 1?	
Why would he describe himself in this way?	
3. What is the main task on which Paul urged the Ephesians to focus their energy? (v. 1)	3. "Calling" (v. 1) refers to the position that we have in Christ, described in chapter 1–3. Since actual practice lags behind position, chapters 4–6 focus on practice.

Explaining the Text	*Examining the Text*
	4. What kinds of actions should result when a person is being humble and patient? (v. 2)
5. Since there is positional unity in the body of Christ because of all we have in common, we must act accordingly.	5. What is the source of the unity that all believers possess? (v. 3)
	6. What will be the result when believers act in accordance with true unity? (v. 3)
7. Notice that all three members of the Godhead contribute to believers' unity. This unity could only come through the sovereign act of God and could not be generated by humans.	7. What do all believers have in common as members of Christ? (vv. 4-6)

B. DIVERSITY BASED ON CHRIST'S GIFTS *(Eph. 4:7-10).* Believers have much in common, but each person is unique. Christ, who came to earth to die, rise again, and take His place as Ruler of the universe, has given each of us special gifts of grace which enable us to serve.

Examining the Text	*Explaining the Text*
1. Read Ephesians 4:7-10. What determined the allocation of grace that has been given to each believer? (v. 7)	1. "Grace" (v. 7) is sometimes translated "gifts of grace," referring to the special enabling for service given uniquely to every believer.
2. Who has received this special endowment for service? (v. 7)	
3. What two benefits come to believers as a result of Christ's resurrection from the dead? (v. 8)	3. When Christ rose (ascended) victorious over death, He brought with Him all those who were captives of sin and death.
4. How does Christ's willingness to come to earth and die (vv. 9-10), set an example of humility and service for us? (cp. 4:2-3)	4. While ascending and descending could refer to coming to earth, they probably mean burial in death (descending) and resurrection (ascending).

C. GROWTH OF THE BODY THROUGH MINISTRY *(Eph. 4:11-16).* Some have received key leadership gifts so that they can help others develop their gifts of service. It is important that each Christian serves to help build up the church, until everyone is mature, and each Christian knows and practices Bible principles. This will promote growth and maturity in the body of Christ.

Explaining the Text	*Examining the Text*
1. These gifts of leadership are important to the church. Apostles and prophets were foundational (Eph. 2:20), with evangelists and pastor/teachers subsequently fulfilling parallel functions.	1. Read Ephesians 4:11-16. What are the four kinds of leadership gifts mentioned in verse 11?
2. God's people are the body of Christ. The body is made up of all who believe on Christ.	2. What is the task of those who have gifts of leadership? (v. 12)
3. Verse 12 describes the purpose of spiritual gifts, verse 13 the goal, and verses 14-16 the result of their use.	3. What happens to the body of Christ when God's people are prepared for and doing works of service? (v. 12)
4. Notice that Jesus Christ is the standard of excellence.	4. What two goals challenge believers to use their gifts of ministry? (v. 13)

Examining the Text	Explaining the Text
5. Describe the result when Christians consistently use their ministry gifts (v. 13).	
6. What is the main characteristic of an immature believer? (v. 14)	6. There are individuals who actively seek to deceive believers.
7. What is the main characteristic of a mature believer? (v. 15)	
8. What happens to Christ's body when Christians minister regularly? (v. 16)	8. The body only achieves maximum potential when every individual part of that body functions effectively.

Experiencing the Text

1. What kinds of actions contribute to maintaining the unity that we have as believers?

Experiencing the Text

2. What should it mean in our churches if each of us has been given a special enabling for service?

3. How would following the example of Christ, who willingly sacrificed Himself for us, change relationships in our churches?

4. In your church, who has been given leadership gifts and how are they being exercised?

5. What role do you play in building up the body of Christ?

Ephesians 4:17-32

Believers Living Holy Lives

One characteristic of our society is the incredible bombardment with media advertising. Every day we are subjected to thousands of brief, penetrating messages designed to captivate and motivate us. Each one has been conceived and implemented to be as effective as possible. Advertisers want to stake out a claim in the corners of our minds so that we will look favorably on their products when it comes time to make a purchase. Better yet, they would like us to decide to make a purchase even if we had not previously thought that we needed their product.

I find the strategies and techniques that they employ fascinating, and instructive. When I was in seminary, my roommate observed that I was the only person he knew who read magazines for the advertisements instead of the articles. While some may avoid TV commercials, I thoroughly enjoy analyzing them. Often they exhibit more originality and creativity than the shows which they interrupt. Certainly more money is spent per minute in production than on most entertainment shows.

One of the techniques that seems to have fallen into disfavor in recent years is the "before and after" testimonial. Perhaps this is due to the potential abuse of such a technique. One of my sons critiqued a before/after advertisement for a diet program. He observed that the "before" photo was poorly lit, out of focus, the person looked sad, and was dressed in sloppy clothing. In the "after" photo the lighting and focus were excellent, the person was well-groomed, smiling, and dressed fashionably. My son observed that the difference was more in the photo than in the person.

One area where the before/after technique should be totally valid is our Christian experience. The quality of life after conversion should show a radical departure from our old lives. Paul paints a graphic word-picture of the Christian's "before and after" experience in the second half of chapter four.

A. CHARACTERISTICS OF OUR OLD LIFE *(Eph. 4:17-19).* Christians should no longer live as they did when they were unsaved. Their minds were ineffective due to hardening their hearts to God, and they were driven to participate in evil behavior.

Examining the Text	*Explaining the Text*
1. Read Ephesians 4:17-19. What does the phrase, "no longer live as the Gentiles do," tell you about the Ephesians' lifestyle prior to Paul's letter? (v. 17)	1. Throughout this section of the letter, Paul uses the word *Gentile* to describe the Ephesians before salvation. However, *Gentile* can be understood more generally as a reference to anyone who lives in rebellion against God.
2. What traits are characteristic of what Paul calls "Gentile thinking"? (vv. 17-18)	
3. Describe the relationship between a "hardened heart," "ignorance," and "darkened understanding" (v. 18).	3. When a person rejects God (hardens his heart), there is logical and inevitable progression downward.
4. What is the result of a hardened heart? (v. 19)	4. The phrase, "having lost all sensitivity," is a description of the result (consequence) of earlier attitudes.

Explaining the Text	Examining the Text
	5. In verse 19, Paul summarizes the pagan lifestyle. List the three words that characterize this lifestyle (v. 19).
	6. In what ways does Gentile society, as described in verses 17-19, appear similar to modern society?

B. CONTRAST WITH NEW LIFE *(Eph. 4:20-24).* Believers came to know Christ through understanding and accepting the truth. And this truth included instruction on how we ought to live. This means turning our backs on our old style of life, and being made new creatures, modeled after God in righteousness and holiness.

Explaining the Text	Examining the Text
	1. Read Ephesians 4:20-24. What is referred to by the phrase "that way"? (v. 20)
2. Ultimately, it is the proclamation of the Word (whether by teaching, preaching, or personal sharing) that leads a person to Christ.	2. What *was* the way in which the Ephesians came to know Christ? (v. 21)

Examining the Text	*Explaining the Text*
3. What are the characteristics (motivations, drives, and attitudes) of the "old self"? (v. 22)	
4. How should a person act when God has given him or her a new mind? (v. 24)	4. When a person becomes a Christian, his whole life (worldview, thought processes, actions, attitudes, etc.) is changed. Before, his life was characterized by futility and darkness. Now, his mind is made new, enabling him to understand truth and reality.

C. CULTIVATING GODLY ACTIONS AND ATTITUDES *(Eph. 4:25-32)*. As believers, we are to lead lives characterized by godly behavior in five different areas. These include telling the truth, controlling anger, not stealing, talking in a wholesome manner, and avoiding improper attitudes and speech. Instead we should be kind, compassionate, and forgiving.

Examining the Text	*Explaining the Text*
1. Read Ephesians 4:25-32. The word *therefore* points back to the verses immediately preceding it. Summarize the main points of the previous passage (vv. 20-24).	1. Verses 25-32 contain six exhortations. Each begins with a negative command (do not....) followed by its positive counterpart (you must....), and then ends with the reason or purpose of the command.

Explaining the Text	*Examining the Text*
	2. What should a Christian stop doing and start doing? (v. 25)
	What is the reason for this command? (v. 25)
3. Apparently there is a valid time for anger, but it must not be prolonged or "nursed along."	3. What are the proper and improper ways of handling anger? (v. 26)
	What is the reason for this approach to anger? (v. 27)
4. We often think of working to meet our own material needs, but Paul greatly expands this concept.	4. How should Christians act and not act regarding material possessions? (v. 28)

Examining the Text	*Explaining the Text*
What is the reason for this attitude toward material possessions? (v. 28)	
5. What should and should not characterize a Christian's talk? (v. 29)	5. Notice, in all of these exhortations, Paul stresses that we do *not* live in a vacuum; what we do affects others.
What will be the result of proper conversation? (v. 29)	
6. The final exhortation, verses 29-32, seems especially relevant for today's churches. What will be the result of relationships characterized by bitterness (rage), anger, brawling, slander, and malice? (v. 30)	6. These six modes of improper behavior are highly relevant: bitterness (animosity, jealousy); rage (outbursts of temper); anger (prolonged anger, grudge); brawling (shouting, arguing); slander (injuring reputation, gossip); malice (ill will, hoping for another's hurt).
What positive actions should characterize our relationships? (v. 32)	

Experiencing the Text

1. What specific things can you do to keep from hardening your heart and losing sensitivity?

2. What role should the Word of God play in our lives today?

3. Why do you think that many who claim to be Christians seem to think and act more like "Gentiles" than new creatures in Christ?

4. Reread the six exhortations in 4:25-32. Which ones are most needed in our churches?

Experiencing the Text

5. Take a few minutes to pray and ask God to help you understand which of these exhortations apply most directly to you. Write down how you want God to help you deal with these problems.

Ephesians 5:1-14

Believers Living Morally Pure Lives

A Christian friend of mine wanted to live for Christ. And she wanted to share what Jesus Christ meant to her with her friends and coworkers. Unfortunately she worked for a company that did not look kindly on religious conversations at work.

This company had a policy that forbid it's employees to discuss politics or religion at work. And each employee was asked to agree, at the time of employment, to abide by this policy. My friend knew that as a Christian, she had to keep her promise.

But my friend still wanted to share Christ with her coworkers. Her problem was compounded by the fact that she commuted a great distance by bus and therefore had no contact with her work friends outside of work hours. And so she prayed that somehow God would give her an opportunity to talk to her friends about Jesus Christ.

One day as she was leaving work, another employee approached her asking if they could talk. This person was facing major problems in her life and felt as though she couldn't cope. She said that she could tell my friend was different from the others who worked there. She didn't know what made my friend different, but knew she wanted what my friend had.

And so the two of them stopped in a nearby restaurant for a cup of coffee and a life-transforming conversation. In the restaurant, after work, my friend was able to lead her coworker to Christ and still remain true to her word. The long ride home seemed short that night as my friend rejoiced in God's answer to her prayer.

In this passage, Paul reminds us that we who have accepted Christ are the visible representations of Christ in this world. We are to shine as lights illuminating a dark world. And as we shine as lights, we will see the results in our lives and the lives of others.

A. WALK IN LOVE *(Eph. 5:1-2).*   Believers are admonished to model their lives after God, and to practice love, just as Jesus Christ who willingly gave Himself for us.

Examining the Text	*Explaining the Text*
1. Read Ephesians 5:1-2. Who is the One that believers should imitate? (v. 1)	1. In these verses, as in the previous section, the word translated "live" (NIV) is the Greek word *peripateo*, meaning "to walk."
2. What relationship with God do we experience that enables us to imitate Him? (v. 1)	
3. How is the example of Jesus Christ more tangible and understandable than the example of God the Father? (v. 2)	3. Since we cannot see God the Father, Jesus Christ models love for us. To most people, God is not a tangible example.
4. What spiritual activities will help us understand how Christ lived so that we can look to Him as our example?	
5. What did it mean for Jesus Christ to express His love for us? (v. 2)	5. "Fragrant offering" (v. 2) refers to the Old Testament sacrificial system where a sacrifice was a pleasant aroma to God because it indicated the offerer's faith.

B. WALK IN MORAL PURITY *(Eph. 5:3-6).*   God's children should avoid all sexual impurity and also other vices, and instead be characterized by thanksgiving. Only those who have been cleansed by God can be part of God's kingdom; the others are doomed to wrath.

Explaining the Text	*Examining the Text*
1. Our language reflects our culture's social values. Today, many equate love with sex. "Love" (v. 2) is sacrificing for another's benefit. Paul clearly taught that sexual immorality is the opposite of love.	1. Read Ephesians 5:3-6. List the kinds of behavior that are inappropriate for believers according to verses 3-6.
	2. How does giving thanks (expressing appreciation) contrast with the vices listed in verses 3 and 4?
3. Verse 5 does not refer to a person who periodically sins, but one driven by idolatry. Such a person has not accepted Christ's sacrifice (5:2).	3. What motivates the person whom Paul describes as an idolater? (v. 5)
4. Apparently there were some who falsely taught that you could *say* you followed Christ but *do* anything you wanted (5:6).	4. Rather than inheriting eternal life ("kingdom of Christ and of God"), what will be the end reward of idolaters? (v. 6)

C. WALK IN THE LIGHT *(Eph. 5:7-14).*   Neither should Christians join with others in sin as in the past. We now should shine forth as light, demonstrating God-honoring behavior. Rather than participating in sin, we should expose it, which will happen as the light that has lighted us shines out through us.

Examining the Text	*Explaining the Text*
1. Read Ephesians 5:7-14. What should be a Christian's attitude toward false teachers and those who rationalize sin? (v. 7)	1. Due to the page layout of the NIV, 5:7 appears to go with 5:6. The Greek construction indicates that it introduces 5:8-14.
2. What do you think it means when Paul says that once believers were darkness but now they are light? (v. 8)	
3. What should be the outcome of living as children of light? (v. 9)	3. Paul uses an agricultural analogy with light, as a plant, bearing good fruit. Darkness (5:11), by contrast, bears no fruit.
4. How can we find out what pleases the Lord? (v. 10)	

Explaining the Text	*Examining the Text*
	5. What should be a believer's attitude toward the fruitless deeds of darkness? (5:11)
6. Apparently the "light" Paul is referring to is spiritual truth demonstrated by consistent behavior of Christians.	6. What is it that exposes the deeds of those who are ungodly, living disobedient lives? (vv. 13-14)
7. Before we accepted Jesus' gift of salvation (eternal life), all of us were dead in our sins.	7. In what way has light (truth) awakened, or made alive, a believer in Christ? (v. 14)

Experiencing the Text

1. What spiritual activities can we pursue that will help us better understand the example Christ set for us?

2. If Christ's love extended even to giving His life for us, what should loving each other mean to us today?

Experiencing the Text

3. What should be the relationship between what we claim to believe and the way we act and behave?

What can you do that will help you live what you believe?

4. How can we shine as light in the world and yet not drive away those who live in darkness?

5. What can we do to evaluate the quality of our lives and determine if indeed we are bearing the fruit of light?

Ephesians 5:15-33

Believers Living Spirit-Filled Lives—Part One

One of the curious characteristics of human nature is the tendency to manifest the pendulum effect. This occurs when a person alternates from one extreme to another, rather than finding the balance point between the two extremes.

I have a friend who had been a pretty good athlete when he was younger. But the responsibilities of family and vocation, combined with too much food and too little exercise, had taken their toll. One summer day I saw him laboring down the street puffing like an asthmatic water buffalo. He was soaked with perspiration and glowed a brilliant shade of red. Between gasps he informed me that he had decided to get back into shape and had just run five miles. From the extreme of a sedentary life, he had swung, like a pendulum, to the other extreme—fitness fanatic.

One college student that I know had a reputation for being deeply involved in school activities, except for studying. When it was time to work on a play, social, or other project, this young man was a leader. But scholarship and his name rarely occurred in the same sentence—at least not with a positive reference. However after his freshman year at college he took a course in philosophy and he hasn't been the same since. All at once he wanted to read all the philosophy books within reach and discuss philosophy with anyone in earshot. The pendulum effect struck again!

People frequently go to extremes when discussing Paul's instructions to families. Some distort Paul's teaching to promote suppression of women or other groups. Others argue just as vehemently to try to explain away Paul's teachings. What we need is balance. Every one of us functions in a variety of relationships. In order to experience God's blessing, we must look for ways to promote others, rather than ourselves. Fighting for our rights is carnality. Relinquishing them (submitting) for the good of others is spirituality.

A. LIVING IN SPIRIT-FILLED SUBMISSION *(Eph. 5:15-21)*. Each Christian should live carefully and wisely before God. Just as a drunk person is controlled by liquor, we should allow the Holy Spirit to control our lives. We demonstrate this control by the way we speak to each other, the way we speak to God, an attitude of thanksgiving, and submitting to others.

Examining the Text	*Explaining the Text*
1. Read Ephesians 5:15-21. How should believers live? (v. 15)	1. The admonition to live (walk) carefully, introduces the verses included in studies 10 and 11.
2. What do you think it means to live as a wise person rather than a foolish person? (v. 15)	
3. How does the exhortation to make the most of every opportunity "because the days are evil" (v. 16) relate to verses 11-14?	3. Apparently God is reminding believers through Paul that life here on earth has a purpose: we are to influence/minister to others.
4. According to verse 18, what should and should not control our lives?	

Explaining the Text	*Examining the Text*
5. Verses 19-21 give four characteristics of one who is living a Spirit-filled life.	5. What should characterize our verbal communication with each other? (v. 19)
6. Notice that singing is a heart response. Even those who think they can't sing aloud, can sing in their hearts.	6. To whom should spiritual music be directed? (v. 19)
	7. What should be our attitude toward all circumstances that we encounter? (v. 20)
8. As an expression of spiritual maturity, every believer is to submit in certain relationships. Submitting is placing another's welfare or preferences ahead of our own.	8. What attitude should we have toward others if we are truly Spirit-filled? (v. 21)

B. BEHAVIOR OF SPIRIT-FILLED WIVES *(Eph. 5:22-24)*.   A wife should submit to her husband as evidence of her serving God. For the husband is head of his wife as Christ is head of the church. Even as the church submits to Christ, so should a spirit-filled wife submit to her own husband.

Examining the Text	*Explaining the Text*
1. Read Ephesians 5:22-24. When a wife places her husband's welfare ahead of her own, to whom is she really submitting? (v. 22)	1. A wife demonstrates spiritual maturity by placing her husband's welfare ahead of her own. This is a decision she makes, not something her husband forces her to do.
2. Why should a wife submit to her own husband? (v. 23)	2. The first New Testament occurrence of the word *submit* is Luke 2:51 when Jesus subordinated His personal preference to His parents'.
3. What is the parallel between a husband and Christ? (v. 23)	3. Headship and submission do not imply superiority and inferiority. They explain functional relationships as a student submits to a teacher. This passage does not imply that all women should submit to all men, but describes relationships in a given marriage.
4. As the Head of the church, what did Christ do for the church, His body? (v. 23)	
5. What is the parallel between a wife and the church? (v. 24)	5. The church submits to Christ by accepting His sacrifice and then looking to Him for continued guidance and blessing.

C. BEHAVIOR OF SPIRIT-FILLED HUSBANDS *(Eph. 5:25-33).* A husband who is Spirit-filled will love his wife as Christ loved the church, giving Himself so that He could help it reach its full potential. Also a husband should love his wife as he loves his own body and cares for it, because she is part of his body. Just as there is a profound relationship between Christ and the church, so also must a husband and wife relate.

Explaining the Text

Examining the Text

1. Just as Ephesians 5:22-24 explains how wives "submit...out of reverence for Christ" (v. 21), so this section explains how husbands "submit...out of reverence for Christ" (v. 21).

1. Read Ephesians 5:25-33. How does a husband "submit" himself to his wife? (v. 25; cp. 5:21)

2. Notice that Christ's purpose was to serve the church, and He used His position to submit to her welfare.

2. How did Jesus show His love for the church? (v. 25)

3. What are some of the things that Christ has done in helping the church to reach it's full potential? (vv. 26-27)

4. It is normal and natural for a man to care for, nurture, and protect his own body.

4. In addition to loving his wife as Christ loved the church, how else is a husband to love his wife? (v. 28)

Examining the Text	*Explaining the Text*
5. Why should a husband treat his wife as if she were part of his own body? (vv. 29-30)	5. Paul draws a parallel between Christ and the church to explain the husband/wife relationship.
6. What are some of the implications of a husband and wife being one flesh, especially regarding the quality and duration of the marriage relationship?	6. Verse 31 probably refers back to the truth of Genesis 2:18-25.
7. What instruction explains how the one flesh, husband/wife relationship should function? (v. 33)	
8. How does Paul summarize his advice to husbands and wives? (v. 33)	

Experiencing the Text

1. How can we specifically practice the four qualities of the Spirit-filled life? (5:19-21)

Experiencing the Text

2. How does our submitting to one another help demonstrate to unbelievers what God expects from everyone?

3. What are some practical ways in which a wife can relate to her husband as the church relates to Christ?

4. What are some practical ways in which a husband can love his wife as Christ loved the church, and as he loves his own body?

5. What do you think would be the consequences if both husband and wife submitted to one another as Paul instructs in verses 22-33?

6. Reread Ephesians 5:15-33 and write several sentences summarizing what you understand these verses teach us about living a Spirit-filled life.

Ephesians 6:1-9

Believers Living Spirit-Filled Lives—Part Two

One of the most important concerns for any society is guiding children into mature, productive adulthood. This means helping them develop appropriate values to guide them in making good judgments and decisions. So-called delinquent behavior is inappropriate and harmful to themselves and others.

But in order to prevent delinquent behavior, we must identify contributing factors. Then we can help children mature positively, rather than encouraging antisocial behavior. The difficulty lies in determining what contributes to delinquent behavior and finding ways to help parents relate appropriately with children.

In the second quarter of the twentieth century, a husband/wife team at a major university did a longitudinal study of delinquent behavior observing growing children repeatedly to record trends and changes. Drs. Sheldon and Eleanor Gleuck analyzed children as they progressed from infancy to adulthood. As a result of years of study they were able to isolate factors contributing to delinquent behavior. By observing a pre-school child in his environment, they could predict teen delinquent behavior with almost 95 percent accuracy.

The researchers found that the style of discipline, particularly from the father, was the key factor in predicting delinquent behavior. Of the three styles they identified —strict, moderate, and lax—they found that moderate (consistent) discipline was best. Surprisingly, they found that strict discipline was the worst. Because strict discipline often is harsh, and because consistency is so difficult with strict discipline, it usually proves counterproductive. And so the children become discouraged and give up.

In this passage, Paul has much to say to parents about ways they relate to children. And he also speaks to us about other relationships.

A. BEHAVIOR OF SPIRIT-FILLED CHILDREN *(Eph. 6:1-3).* Children must obey their parents even as God commanded through Moses, promising that this is the only way to enjoy a long and profitable life.

Examining the Text	*Explaining the Text*
1. Read Ephesians 6:1-3. In what sense could it be considered right for children to obey their parents? (v. 1)	1. Proper behavior of children is part of their obligation to God ("in the Lord").
2. How do obedience (v. 1) and honoring father and mother (v. 2) fit together with a child's obligation to God?	
3. What are the expected outcomes of obeying the command in verse 2?	3. While the second commandment (Ex. 20:5-6) includes a general consequence, this is the first commandment with a specific promise.
4. What are the implied consequences of a disobedient, undisciplined life? (v. 3)	

B. BEHAVIOR OF SPIRIT-FILLED PARENTS *(Eph. 6:4)*.   Parents should rear their children with God's training and instruction and not exasperate them.

Explaining the Text	*Examining the Text*
1. "Fathers" are addressed not because they alone are responsible, rather Paul selected them because of their leadership responsibility (5:23-24).	1. Read Ephesians 6:4. What are some things that fathers can do to ensure that children are brought up in the training and instruction of the Lord?
	2. What kinds of parental attitudes and actions would tend to exasperate (provoke to anger) children?
3. "Training" (nurture) includes guidance, direction, and encouragement. "Instruction" (admonition) more emphasizes correction.	3. How do guiding (training) and correcting (instruction) both play a part in child-rearing?
	4. In what sense should rearing our children come from God? (v. 4)

C. BEHAVIOR OF SPIRIT-FILLED WORKERS *(Eph. 6:5-8).* Slaves should respond to their masters as they would to Christ, not just to please them but to honor God. They should work knowing that God ultimately will reward.

Examining the Text	*Explaining the Text*
1. Read Ephesians 6:5-8. What attitude should workers have as they serve their employers? (v. 5)	1. Slaves (also translated servants) had little personal freedom. They had some things in common with workers today, though workers have more freedom of choice.
2. Who watches over those working for masters? (v. 6)	
3. What explanation does Paul give for his exhortation to serve appropriately? (vv. 6-7)	3. Obviously a slave would want his master to think well of him, but Paul goes beyond this in suggesting higher motivation.
4. What is the end result, or outcome, of faithful serving? (v. 8)	
5. Based on verses 5-8, what appropriate guidelines could you suggest for workers today?	

D. BEHAVIOR OF SPIRIT-FILLED MASTERS *(Eph. 6:9).*   Paul ends this section with an exhortation to masters. A Spirit-filled master must treat his slaves sensitively, knowing that God is their Master and He does not play favorites.

Explaining the Text	*Examining the Text*
1. This is the sixth category of individuals to whom Paul explains the application of his command to "Submit to one another" (5:21).	1. Read Ephesians 6:9. What is referred to by the phrase, "in the same way"? (v. 9)
	2. What reasons does Paul give for not threatening slaves (workers)? (v. 9)
	3. What do you think Paul would say about the use of intimidation or coercion in motivating workers?
4. Notice that Paul never implies that Christ removes differences in position or function. He does state that all should be valued equally as persons.	4. How does the last phrase in verse 9 fit together with verse 8?

Experiencing the Text

1. What can parents do to help their children follow God's instructions to them in this passage?

2. What suggestions can you offer to help parents avoid exasperating their children?

What kinds of activities would help bring children up in the training and instruction of the Lord?

3. In what ways are today's workers both similar to, and different from, slaves?

4. What suggestions could you give to employers (supervisors) to help them effectively lead those who report to them?

Experiencing the Text

5. Reread Ephesians 6:1-9. Then write down all the general guidelines for relationships that you can find in these verses?

Ephesians 6:10-24

Believers Living with Spiritual Power

When our first son was very young, Elaine and I discussed those traits that we wanted to cultivate in our children (and in ourselves too). At the top of our list was honesty. If our sons could learn to be honest with God, with us, and others, then they could be honest with themselves too. And so we worked at encouraging this and other character traits.

Interestingly enough, we soon discovered that many of the values we were trying to teach sometimes seemed contradictory. We wanted them to be honest always, but were horrified when one of our sons told a hostess in a home where we were visiting that she "must be the fattest person in the whole wide world." And so we had to teach discretion. It is wrong to lie, but that doesn't mean you have to tell everything you think.

We wanted our sons to be creative and imaginative in approaching tasks and opportunities. But it soon became obvious that school teachers, and many others in positions of responsibility place a higher value on conformity and compliance that on creativity and innovation. And so we confronted the task of trying to stimulate our sons to view life with freshness, but also to avoid "rocking the boat" needlessly.

Nowhere does the tension become more obvious than when teaching both independence and cooperation. We all need to work and function as strong, self-sufficient individuals. God has given us many resources to use for His glory. And yet we also are members of the body of Christ— accountable to, and responsible for, each other. None of us is an island.

In this final section of Ephesians, Paul stresses both aspects of the Christian life. God provides us with resources to conquer Satan in his attacks. But we do not have to stand alone. The rest of the body of Christ should assist us as we strive to live victoriously.

A. EQUIPPED FOR SPIRITUAL CONFLICT *(Eph. 6:10-17)*.   In order to
be strong we need to arm ourselves against Satan. Since we are engaged
in spiritual battle, we need to be armed with truth, righteousness, a
foundation for our feet, a shield, a helmet, and a sword.

Examining the Text	*Explaining the Text*
1. Read Ephesians 6:10-17. What is the source of a believer's strength? (v. 10)	
2. What are several reasons why a Christian needs to wear spiritual armor? (vv. 11-13)	2. The armor that Paul refers to as he describes spiritual preparation is that which was worn by the Roman soldiers.
3. Why is personal honesty important in standing against Satan? (v. 14)	3. Truth refers to telling the truth. Righteousness is the quality of righteous or holy living.
4. What does righteous living mean to a believer? (v. 14)	
5. Why is peace important to a believer engaged in spiritual battle? (v. 15)	5. Having feet shod is for the purpose of standing firm with stability, not for moving forward.

Explaining the Text	Examining the Text
6. The actual shield that quenches the darts is faith itself.	6. What part does faith play in our defense against Satan and his attacks? (v. 16)
	7. How does salvation protect or influence our minds? (v. 17)
8. The sword is the only offensive element in this listing of the Christian's armor. Practical knowledge of the Bible is our best offense.	8. Why is the Word of God important to each and every believer? (v. 17)

B. SUPPORTING OTHERS IN SPIRITUAL CONFLICT *(Eph. 6:18-20)*. We do not stand alone, but are responsible to pray for others so that they also can live effectively. Paul especially wanted believers to pray for him so that he would proclaim the Gospel boldly as a good ambassador.

Explaining the Text	Examining the Text
1. Even with all of the armor listed in these verses, believers still are not self-sufficient. We need each other.	1. Read Ephesians 6:18-20. What part does prayer play in successfully withstanding Satan's attacks? (v. 18)

Examining the Text	Explaining the Text
2. What do you think Paul meant when he admonished the believers to be alert? (v. 18)	
3. What did Paul want his fellow believers to pray about for him? (vv. 19-20)	3. Paul's conclusion was based on his awareness of the fact that he was not self-sufficient, but strongly needed prayer support from believers.
What is the importance of praying for these same requests for other Christians today?	

C. CONCLUSION AND BLESSING *(Eph. 6:21-24).* Tychicus was to share Paul's condition with the Ephesians (probably while delivering the letter) and to encourage them with a personal word. Paul concludes by desiring that the Ephesians experience the peace, grace, and love of God.

Examining the Text	Explaining the Text
1. Read Ephesians 6:21-24. What were some personal qualities of Tychicus? (v. 21)	1. Tychicus often labored with Paul, frequently as a messenger. Apparently, it was his job to deliver this letter to the Ephesians.

Explaining the Text	*Examining the Text*
	2. What things did Paul want Tychicus to do for him in relating to the Ephesian believers? (vv. 21-22)
	3. How would knowing of Paul's condition encourage the believers?
4. Paul often mentioned grace and peace in the introductions to his letters.	4. What spiritual qualities, in addition to grace and peace, are mentioned by Paul in verses 23-24?

Experiencing the Text

1. How should we prepare ourselves in daily life if we recognize that we are engaged in spiritual battle?

2. What do we need to do in order to use the Sword of the Spirit effectively in battle?

Experiencing the Text

3. What can Christians do to help and encourage each other to stand strong in spiritual battle?

4. How can we be more faithful and effective in praying for fellow believers?

5. How is Tychicus a good model, or example, for us to follow?

6. Based on what you have learned from the Epistle to the Ephesians, what specific areas would you like to ask God to strengthen in your life?